Charles Faudree's
French Country Signature

CHARLES FAUDREE'S
French Country Signature

Charles Faudree with M. J. Van Deventer

Photographs by Jenifer Jordan

Gibbs Smith, Publisher
Salt Lake City

First Edition

07 06 05 04   7 6 5

Published by

Gibbs Smith, Publisher

P.O. Box 667

Layton, Utah 84041

Orders: (1-800) 748-5439

www.gibbs-smith.com

Designed and produced by Kurt Wahlner

Printed and bound in Hong Kong

Library of Congress Cataloging-in-Publication Data

Faudree, Charles.

Charles Faudree's French country signature / Charles Faudree with
M. J. Van Deventer ; photographs by Jenifer Jordan.—1st ed.

p. cm.

ISBN 1-58685-288-4

1. Faudree, Charles. 2. Interior decoration—United
States—History—20th century. 3. Decoration and ornament,
Rustic—France—Influence. I. Van Deventer, M. J. II. Title.

DEDICATED TO READERS, CLIENTS AND FRIENDS who have
graciously shared my love of design and interiors. Every
house is different, from contemporary to country, but in
each is a French translation we all love.

Table Des Matières

Contents

Previously published in Traditional Home *magazine.*

Merci

ACKNOWLEDGEMENTS

WHETHER IT'S BEEN A DREAM or a goal, I have always wanted to do a book before I was too old to remember all the pleasures of decorating other people's homes, as well as my own. I am so pleased this book has finally come to pass, with everyone's help.

I particularly want to thank and remember my mother for always allowing me to express myself, starting when I was only ten years old. She let me choose the color for the front door. It was a Dutch door with shutters and I got to paint it every year in whatever color I chose ~ Wedgwood blue, pink, apple green. I got that out of my system early on in my design career. Now I much prefer black.

I wish to offer my heartfelt thanks to the many people who helped make this book possible. I am especially indebted to the homeowners who graciously allowed us to enter their private worlds so we could share their homes with you. They include Joanne Hearst Castro, Leigh Farrar, Leigh Ann and Frank Fore, Dru and Michael Hammer, Mickey and Tom Harris, Judy and Paul Kantor, Julie and Warren Kruger, Patricia and Cleber Massey, Carol Pielsticker, Tracy and Hal Salisbury, Peter Walter and Holbrook Webb.

Thanks also to

Jenifer Jordan, photographer, for her beautiful photographs and for being ever so patient with me.

Nancy E. Ingram, photo stylist, for being my agent, president of my fan club and my dear friend.

M. J. Van Deventer, writer, for the wonderful words, for completing my sentences for so many years and for always making me sound better.

Jim Steinmeyer, illustrator, for the beautiful drawings and for being my closest friend.

Shawn Lovejoy and April Moore, my assistants, who took on extra responsibilities while I was involved with the book.

Cathy Keating and Tracy Salisbury, cheerleaders, who persistently encouraged me to do a book.

And finally, Madge Baird, editor, who has kept us on the path toward meeting the deadline and fruition of this project.

Charles Faudree

11

In a library, an Empire mahogany armchair features bronze trim and flanks a coffee table accented with a pair of candlesticks, a crystal decanter, fresh flowers in a silver vase and part of a collection of English and French pocket watches.

Avant-Propos
FOREWORD

AT TRADITIONAL HOME, we do not keep statistics on how often a particular interior designer appears in the magazine. If we did, I can tell you ~ without hesitation ~ whose name would have the most stories next to it: Charles Faudree. I don't have to thumb through my shelf of past issues or conduct a search of our electronic database to confirm this fact. It's just something all of us at the magazine know.

We also know that whenever we feature a house Charles has designed, we will receive many gleeful letters of thanks from our readers. To say that Charles is a favorite of *Traditional Home* readers is a huge understatement. If it is possible to conduct a love affair without ever meeting or speaking, our readers and Charles Faudree have been carrying on for years. We're merely the go-betweens.

Of course, we have our own special affection for Charles and his decorating. In 1995, we presented him with a *Traditional Home* Design Award for innovation and excellence in traditional style. During the course of our eight-year Design Award program, we honored almost fifty interior designers and architects, some who were quite famous, and others who were appearing in a national publication for the first time. The funny thing about giving Charles one of our awards was that it seemed redundant. Anyone familiar with *Traditional Home* already knew how highly we regarded his exuberant take on French Country style.

Several years ago, as we celebrated our tenth anniversary, we handpicked eight interior designers whose work we admired and asked them to appear in a book with our name on it. *Traditional Home Signature Style* presented visions of beauty in rooms and houses all across the country. Do I have to tell you the name of the designer whose chapter led off the book? Charles Faudree. Naturally.

As you will see in the pages of the book you are holding, Charles has a wonderful way with a room. He infuses a space with freshness and vitality, making it elegant and inviting ~ but most of all, personal. If you don't know it already, you will soon learn that Charles enjoys buying and selling his own houses (now that's a true understatement). In each home ~ and in an amazingly short amount of time ~ Charles puts his own stamp on the place. Every one of his houses is uniquely his ~ replete with his prodigious collections, spilling over with comfort and exuding a sense of his having lived there forever.

Today, as I write this, *Traditional Home* is purchased and read by more people than any other upscale shelter and decorating magazine in America. Now, I'm not going to tell you that we have arrived at this proud distinction because we have published so many houses designed by Charles Faudree.

Then again, it certainly didn't hurt.

~ Ann Omvig Maine
Editor in Chief, *Traditional Home* magazine
February 2003

Introduction
INTRODUCTION

IN THE LANGUAGE OF INTERIOR DESIGN, I would like to think I have helped to elevate French Country to a fine art. It is an excessive, exuberant style that fosters my favorite design principle ~ too much is never enough. I would also like to think I have achieved a reputation for creating settings that have all the elegant accouterments of a French country estate, without any of the traditional French pretentiousness.

The style has its origins in the French countryside, straddling both the southern and northern regions of western Europe and drawing from many influences. Yet my version of French Country style is a colloquial look devoid of any precise boundaries. Always in the vernacular of this style, the name evokes images of farmhouses or small châteaux dotting the genteel French countryside. In our imagination, it is Monet revisited through a myriad of garden paintings, always reflecting the warmth of sunlight and lavender-filled fields.

I believe the style is defined by the furnishings themselves, with each region of France contributing a particular style. Many of the furnishings that make this look so special were used originally in French country châteaux, which were considered less important houses than those maintained in the French cities.

Given my French name and heritage, I have always been drawn, almost charismatically, to the charm of French Country. I am an avowed Francophile and I love the French carving so typical of French Country furnishings. They are not so decorated with ormolu or gilt like some traditional period French pieces. There is a simplicity, a gentle softness to the furnishings I find very calming and soothing. I love the mix of fabrics, blending plaids with florals and old tapestries. French Country is a working-class style and I believe it wears well.

My first informal decorating project was my parents' home in Muskogee, Oklahoma. Of course, I furnished it in a French Provincial style. But it would be more than two decades before decorating and design called to me as a worthy profession.

After graduating from Northeastern State University in Tahlequah, Oklahoma, with a degree in art, a stint at teaching art in Kansas City, Missouri, and a sojourn at the Kansas City Art Institute, I returned to Oklahoma and later moved to Dallas, Texas, working in the realm of home furnishings accessories.

Ironically, I did not begin to design for clients until I was thirty-eight years old. I just felt I wasn't doing anything significant with my life, so I moved back to Muskogee, where my mother, Ruby, and sister, Francie, still lived, and redecorated my sister's home. That was the beginning of a design career that now spans more than twenty-five years.

I took my first trip to Paris, France, when I was twenty-six years old. I truly fell in love with Paris. It was everything ~ the architecture, the most beautiful and sensual language, the flowers, the food, the wines. I haven't missed a year since.

When I opened my interior design studio in Tulsa, Oklahoma, in 1979, I had the good fortune to become recognized quickly for my comfortable and colorful style. Without diluting the visual impact of my French Country style, I tried to make the style easily accessible to my clients, while acquainting them with its charming and endearing qualities. I have continued to decorate every one of my eleven homes, and those of my clients, in a continual evolution of this style.

This changeable landscape of my residences ~ from a New England saltbox, a French-style château and a mid-town atelier to two weekend retreats, is a key to my perpetual desire for change. Early on in my peripatetic moves to new residences, I said in a magazine interview that I feel about my houses the same way Elizabeth Taylor feels about her husbands. Each one is my best and my last. It has become an affectionate query among my friends and clients to ask me if, indeed, each new house will be my last. I happily indulge their benign suspicion.

off each other and off the contrast of the woods. I'm always inspired by new fabrics and I think that's what keeps this particular style fresh.

I'm often asked to define this style, to elaborate on the secret of my French Country signature. I just always say, Oh, it's all in the mix. Hopefully, that mix is always artful, eclectic and inspiring. I believe there is an art to arranging and accessorizing. I try to create what is pleasing to look at, what is appropriate and in balance for the room. It's important to know when to let the eye rest.

But I am a designer who thrives on change and I believe the only perfection is change ~ the continual trial and error of creating new vignettes, new tablescapes, new homes. I readily admit there is a "rush" as I begin each new decorating project ~ my own or those for my appreciative clients.

With a taste for the eclectic, I would like to think I have mastered one of the main tenets of this style ~ combining traditional prints, patterns, colors and textures with just the right furnishings. It's magic the way fabrics play

With my love for mixing past and present, old and new, I like to create inviting rooms that express a casual, comfortable feeling. I am often guided by my belief that there are no rules about where you can use things. That's why French Country design has a pleasing, fluid quality and an appeal that is timeless.

ABOVE

Above the mantel is an elaborate, gilded English mirror. The mantel showcases antique garden urns, holding large bunches of hydrangeas, along with Staffordshire cows. The matching French wingback bergères *have been in five of Charles's homes. The reproduction coffee table is included in the Faudree custom line of signature furniture. Fabric for the windows, sofa and miniature* bergère *is "Florentine Damask" by Beaumont & Fletcher.*

Entrées

ENTRIES

1

The first impression of a home often begins at the front door. Whether painted red to balance the gray-brown of a New England saltbox or pristine white against a gray-blue exterior, the front door is always a welcoming motif in French Country design.

I admired the architectural charm of a 1923 Dutch Colonial house long before I purchased it. Its front-gabled roof, shuttered crank-out windows and window boxes overflowing with begonias and lacy ferns were captivating. If the exterior of a house entices, the interior ~ especially the entryway ~ must enthrall. The wide floorboards and high-pitched ceiling of the Dutch Colonial gave the house a quaint charm.

It is important to decorate a front porch, a porte cochere, or even a back entry to set the tone for the rest of the home. At one entry, I stationed a pair of limestone whippets ~ my business logo ~ to greet guests. Pairs ~ whether it's chairs, mirrors, sconces, topiaries or urns ~ make a powerful impression.

A classic design plan for an entry is to select a magnificent piece of furniture that will make a statement about the home. It can be a table; massive stone urns; a commode graced with an elegant mirror; an antique clock, rug or chandelier; benches laden with needlepoint pillows; or even an inviting chair.

One challenging entry transformation was in an unassuming

LEFT

The 1840s clock in a small entryway was purchased years ago. Barnwood was used on the entry walls and is a great backdrop for the clock. Majolica boots hold a collection of Charles's antique canes.

RIGHT

Heirloom canes provide a clever conversation piece in an entry.

OVERLEAF

Oklahoma Governor's Mansion.

FACING

"The Roost" sign welcomes guests to Charles's weekend retreat.

LEFT

An iron dog drinking fountain welcomes guests and their dogs to his country cabin.

duplex in a prime Tulsa location within a secluded enclave of two 1970s ranch-style duplexes. The exterior was void of any architectural distinction. By creating a two-story entrance hall, the character of the entrance was changed, giving it the look and feel of a tower. A skylight flooded the entryway and panel windows were added to overlook a small French Country-style garden with espaliers climbing the walls. On the outside, the original brick façade was covered with stucco and painted taupe with white trim, creating a nice backdrop for a distinctive old carriage lamp.

Another ambitious entryway was in the Oklahoma Governor's Mansion, a 1920s three-story limestone residence that was restored and refurbished after Governor Frank Keating and his wife, Cathy, assumed their residency in 1994. Seven interior designers worked on the project together. Mrs. Keating has long been an advocate of historic preservation, and she wanted an authentic restoration rather than a wholesale renovation. That required all of the designers to do painstaking historical research. As a result, every room became a treasure, reflecting a sense of the state's history. Among the special touches we added to the entry were a staircase runner featuring the name of every governor since statehood and a replica of the silver punch bowl that was on the *U.S.S. Oklahoma*. It was set on an antique table.

Even a back entry can make guests feel welcome. At The Roost, an antique bench dressed with toile and embroidered pillows invites guests and their canine companions to enjoy the pleasures of a casual weekend.

FAR LEFT

An antique Black Forest carved vase holds wild-flowers on a French garden table in the entry of a weekend cabin.

LEFT

In the country, dogs are as welcome at his cabin as their owners. If the crowd is large, the small entry acts as a second dining room.

Tabletops are as important as the table itself. And this beautiful antique console, itself a treasure, is topped with leather books, antique figurines and a garden urn overflowing with blooms. An entryway, as the home's first impression, says volumes about the rest of the house.

This magnificent entry evokes the era of Louis XV, with its wrought-iron stairway and balustrade. An eighteenth-century Provençal commode is a focal point, flanked by Louis XV carved walnut side chairs. An elegant bronze Napoleon III lantern lights the stairs.

"IF THE EXTERIOR OF A HOUSE
ENTICES, THE INTERIOR ~
ESPECIALLY THE ENTRYWAY ~
MUST ENTHRALL."

The Louis XV commode always moves when
Charles does and the nineteenth-century
blackamoor has greeted his guests in several
previous homes.

LEFT

The home is a mix of traditional and contemporary furnishings and accessories. The scale of the large, antique stone table
works well with the soaring architecture.

BELOW

This contemporary house is designed with all of the rooms
organized off a rear loggia, which allows every room to be
surrounded by light.

Large antique French olive jars lead the eye down the hall toward the nineteenth-century French commode and its display of antique majolica.

Salles de Séjour

LIVING ROOMS

2

Jim Steinmeyer

The rich fullness of furnishings and fabrics and an artful use of symmetry characterize many of the living rooms I design. In the French Country style, they are formal yet wonderfully casual, giving homeowners and guests a feeling of opulence with so much to see. They are overflowing but never cluttered or overpowering, even in the smallest of spaces.

Part of the charm of a living room is a skillful blend of rustic and refined antiques and furnishings, with fabrics, colors, collections and accessories that create a beautiful, cohesive room. Color is the key that blends this rich mix of patterns ~ toile, paisley, stripes, plaids ~ into a visually appealing display.

Consistency in the choice of furnishings has been important throughout my design career. A basic rule is that furnishings have to be antique and preferably of French origin. Being steadfast to this principle keeps redecorating expenses manageable and allows furnishings to be moved to new settings when the occasion dictates.

Recycling is also a part of the design process. Moving often has allowed me to be ready for the next design challenge as soon as the last renovation is complete, and frequently has shown me how to assign new uses, new settings and new clothes for old furnishings.

FACING

The cabin is cozy and encourages great conversation with its close-knit seating areas. It also gives Charles and his friends wonderful views of the wooded setting along a meandering creek.

RIGHT

From the Gustavian period, this nineteenth-century Swedish secrétaire *matches the cabin's rustic spirit. The* secrétaire, *a major focal point in the cabin's living room, displays a French tureen.*

Almost every design project begins with a large pivotal piece, usually of French or English ancestry. It can be a painting, a grand mirror, nineteenth-century French carved wooden urns, or antique mantel clocks. Perhaps the most unusual was an eighteenth-century tole coal stove, which I purchased from an owner who had used it to stash her gin. Just one serious piece of furniture, such as an armoire or chest, will make the rest of the furnishings seem important. Not only will such a piece make a dramatic statement, but it will be used for years, often moving from home to home like a nomad.

In one example, a massive French Country buffet became a focal piece in the living room. Originally that piece was in a kitchen. Ten years ago, you might not have seen that paradoxical use of a piece of furniture in French Country design. But it's that informality and flexibility that is another aspect of the style's charm. In another example, an old stone fireplace surround was purchased in France and brought home for specific use in an outdoor room, but it fit the opening for the living room fireplace and seemed perfect for that space.

From the choice of stellar pieces, the symmetry begins with the addition of complementary curtains, matching chairs and ottomans positioned just so ~ perhaps flanking a fireplace or a game table ~ and small tables providing spaces for conversation and displays of treasured collections.

LEFT

Books form the base for this tablescape—an antique rooster on a pedestal, a neighboring bird cage and a cache pot filled with colorful daisies picked from the yard of a country cabin.

FACING

The living room of Charles's weekend retreat is a study in blue and white and reflects the influence of Sweden in some of the furnishings. The original stone fireplace was replaced with a Louis XVI mantelpiece and matching side cupboards. Chinese-export porcelain vases add interest near the high ceiling. Fabrics featured in the room are "Petit Parc" and "Senanque" by Pierre Frey.

Magnificent windows reach twenty feet high, bringing in the sky. The Directoire **buffet des corps,** *circa 1790, has an immense scale appropriate to the volume of the room with its high ceilings. In the illuminated alcove at the end of the room, a Steinway piano creates a music room setting.*

Small paintings, mirrors, sconces, brackets or ancestral portraits ~ I call them "instant ancestors" ~ will frame a chest or commode or might grace the space above a fireplace mantel. But these arrangements are not static. Following a symmetrical design gives movement and rhythm to the setting, presenting an exciting visual display that moves the eye around the room, then lets it come to rest at well-placed collections.

Much of the joy of decorating comes in the willful juxtaposition of placing an elegant, serious piece of furniture next to a more primitive, rustic one. Or wrapping a new linen fabric on an old chair that has flaking paint and worn carvings. The fun of decorating comes in the mix.

Part of the pleasure in designing living rooms is paying homage to sheer practicality. In my French château-style home, the living room floor was actually stained and scored concrete designed to resemble French tiles ~ it was also very easy to clean. Topping the cola-colored floor with an Oriental carpet gave it a touch of elegance. Of course, my family of King Charles spaniels much preferred to lounge on the chintz-covered living room chairs accessorized with needlepoint and silk pillows. The dogs were only doing their job, keeping the chairs warm for me while I was away.

This home is a perfect example of how well French Country can dress a sleek contemporary home. The dramatic architecture is softened by large-scale French period furnishings mixed with antique and contemporary accessories. Chenille fabric by Coraggio covers the sofas.

ABOVE AND LEFT

This Tuscan-style farmhouse was built forty years ago and the chandelier is original to the house. The two French antique bergère *chairs were purchased in France, along with the two tables at the ends of the sofa. Also found on that trip was an antique bronze bust of a young boy by Augte, a Parisian sculptor. The bust accents an antique Moroccan trunk.*

The large mural behind the sofa is actually a pair of wooden doors that were
found in Paris, part of a large eighteenth-
century room. The coffee table is made
from an antique catafalque. Other tables
in the room are fashioned from antique
Aubusson panels, which are family heir-
looms. The large rug is a custom needlepoint by Stanton. The pivotal fabric in the
room is the Brunschwig & Fils toile
"Sonnet 14."

An eighteenth-century French fruitwood table is right at home under the original leaded-glass window. The table is flanked by a pair of antique French bergères. The footstool features carved ram's feet and another fabric, adding to the mélange of textures and prints used to upholster the room's furnishings.

FACING

This view features a miniature eighteenth-century French bergère wing chair that was a gift to Charles on his fortieth birthday from his sister. The pair of tole sconces over the sofa may look familiar, as they have been photographed in a variety of magazines. A bow-front Louis XV commode from southwestern France sits under the stairs. The reproduction coffee table is included in the Faudree custom line of signature furniture.

In his French château-style home, the room is divided by a center table displaying canine candlesticks, tortoiseshell objects and treasured books. Each side of the room is dressed in a symmetrical but not identical fashion. (Previously published in **Traditional Home** *magazine.)*

THE FLORAL HOME

Leslie Geddes-Brown   THE FLORAL HOME   CROWN

THE FLORAL DECORATOR
KENNETH TURNER

PARIS IN

One of two matching stone chimney breasts features an antique French flag holder. Two Louis XV bergères are covered in casual checks. The sofa is upholstered in "Tole Bougeval" by Pierre Frey. An antique Heriz rug covers the stained-and-scored concrete floor. (Previously published in Traditional Home magazine.)

An example of recycling is apparent in the rendering above. The antique French wing chair and Louis XV sofa are reupholstered for the new setting. The little stool wears its original fabric.

LEFT

In this 20 by 30-foot living room, with the dining room at one end and the living room at the other, a French Country feeling was created using a soft, warm color scheme of ivory walls and creams, reds and greens in a variety of fabric patterns. The home is an ideal showcase for the couple's extensive collection of French furnishings and accessories.

FAR LEFT

The coffee table is an antique French side table with cabriole legs. Other features in the room include a French carved armoire next to the fireplace and a pair of matching chairs flanking a table to create a conversation area. The room is grounded with a custom seagrass rug.

RIGHT

A continental French Country spirit domi-
nates this room. The sofa is custom-made by
Rose Tarlow. The seventeenth-century mirror
is Dutch. The eighteenth-century German
walnut chest was purchased at auction, as
were the lamps, which were originally
eighteenth-century Italian gilt-wood altar
candlesticks. Other special features in the
room include a beechwood chair, a black-
and-gilt Japanese tray table and a pair of
tole jardinières, *all eighteenth-century*
Louis XV.

LEFT

In the same continental flavor, the other
side of the room features an eighteenth-
century Italian, Japanned bureau cabinet,
strategically placed in front of a seven-
teenth-century tapestry from Bruge.
Paintings by Henri Fantin-Latour and
Jean-Baptiste Camille Corot hang above an
eighteenth-century French carved walnut
chest. One of the most unusual treasures is
a blue-and-white collection of seventeenth-
century Chinese porcelain, rescued from a
Dutch vessel that was shipwrecked in 1680.
The cargo was recovered three hundred
years later and the owner purchased it at a
Christie's auction.

A Louis XVI–style stone mantel and **trumeau** is accented with a large ancestral portrait. The symmetrical placement of a collection of plates and matching bronze wall sconces illuminates the mantel. Also included in the room are a Napoleon III lacquer tea table, a Venetian gilt-wood and polychrome torchère and an extensive collection of eighteenth- and nineteenth-century Chinese Canton porcelains in the "Famille Rose" pattern.

ABOVE

Positioned by French doors is a painted Louis XV table a jouet,
a game table, paired with Louis XVI side chairs that were found
in Paris.

LEFT

A Portuguese needlepoint carpet grounds this elegant room,
which features an Italian painted chandelier, a Louis XVI tea
table and a pair of eighteenth-century Italian polychrome urns,
which were converted to custom lamps. Fabric on the sofa and the
curtains is Kimberly chenille by Lee Jofa, in different colorways.

This home originally was built in 1929 for actress Greer Garson. The Louis Valtat painting, Au Salon, truly draws the eye directly to the fireplace and its mantel. It is just one of many fabulous pieces of art in this California home. On the eighteenth-century French commode under the mirror is a signed bronze by Emile Boyer of a child with a dog.

The great hall of this family retreat in the Allegheny Mountains has a towering sandstone fireplace and massive wood beams. The imposing size is balanced by comfortable seating groups arranged for dining, entertaining or intimate conversation. A Brunschwig & Fils deer and glade pattern was chosen for the wing chairs to repeat the woodsy colors of the surrounding forest.

Salons & Bibliothèques

SITTING
ROOMS
& LIBRARIES

3

As much as I love chairs, it seems only natural that they play an important part of the design plan in sitting rooms and grand libraries. These rooms are often in transitional spaces ~ surprise nooks that are a tucked-away setting for a small collection of chairs and a table, an antique desk or a bookcase brimming with books and bibelots.

In some of the homes I've designed, the sitting room is formal yet casual, that eclectic mix that showcases lovely upholstered chairs, ottomans, antique pieces such as a late eighteenth-century French Country server accented with blue-and-white Staffordshire plates, blue-and-white ceramics and bovines. Small tables or chests placed between harmonious chairs are the greatest places to read, to have morning coffee or afternoon tea or enjoy conversations with friends.

At my cabin, a daybed ~ a true French accessory ~ was added to the sitting area, offering guests a place to lounge while enjoying a wonderful view of the creek and nature's ever-changing theater. My bedroom frequently features a small sitting area for relaxing reading. In one home, the bay window in a sitting room between the kitchen and master bedroom acted as a small conservatory. The view of the tiny pool beyond framed the vignette and allowed the furnishings and personal objects to take center stage.

One sitting area served as a transition space between the formal living and dining room. A French fruitwood desk became the focal point, accented by an elaborate, gilded English Regency bull's-eye mirror that was found at an old estate in Tulsa. Bookshelves framed the space, housing embossed leather-bound books to suggest a small library. A tabletop pedestal was a great showpiece for a collection of bronze, pot-metal and terra-cotta dogs. In a recent addition to my sitting room repertoire, a nook was carved out of entryway

The red library is a signature of the designer's French Country style. A sound system hides behind the carved panel in the arched doorway. The walnut chest is in the style of Louis XV. Napoleonic memorabilia, including a statue of the icon himself, graces the doorway. (Previously published in Traditional Home *magazine.)*

"WHATEVER THE DESIGN AND COLOR MOTIF, THESE CHARMING SPACES INVITE REST AND RELAXATION, READING AND REFLECTION."

space, where four people could sit and complete a jigsaw puzzle. Some sitting rooms have grown into grand libraries, brimming with books and memorabilia, especially my Napoleonic treasures in one home. The library was accented with red toile wallpaper and red-and-white check fabrics to create an overall effect of being cozy and inviting.

In a client's home, the original small dining room became a breakfast room –sitting area. The box bay window was original to the house and served to bring the look of nature indoors. Cedar beams and moldings were added to give the room a French Country feeling. The former library became the formal dining room. And the family room received the addition of paneling from old French doors. Bookcases were shuttered with doors from an antique armoire, and for symmetry, where space didn't allow a bookcase, a faux case was created.

In another home, a white-pine-plank ceiling was used to give the suggestion of a converted French farmhouse. A Chinese tea tin was paired with a French café table, placed between provençal-style wingback chairs. Red-and-white-checked curtains and pillows made from beaded tea cozies provided charming accents in the space. Floor-to-ceiling bookcases housed a large collection of design resource books collected through the years, along with the many novels and historical and contemporary autobiographies I enjoy reading.

On a French desk, leather books displayed a bronze relief of Napoleon, a bronze inkwell and miniature military hats. The custom-made lamp was fashioned from a spelter statue of Napoleon on a horse. Dog memorabilia has reigned in some of the libraries; Napoleon has held court in many others.

Whatever the design and color motif, these charming spaces invite rest and relaxation, reading and reflection ~ just the kind of treasured leisure pursuits for which sitting rooms and libraries are created.

*Gathered in this library is the memorabilia of the
Napoleonic empire ~ statues, books, prints, portraits
and epaulettes. Formal wool curtains lined in
striped silk create an elegant look. (Previously published in* **Traditional Home** *magazine.)*

In a sunny sitting area, an antique bench displays needlepoint and Aubusson tapestry cushions with period passementerie.

In this magnificent French home's kitchen area with its cozy fireplace and comfortable furnishings, the cook never feels left out of the conversation.

*A Louis XV limestone fireplace is a focal point
in this library, accented by high ceilings and
surrounded by boiseries, French for paneled walls.
The Aubusson-style carpet adds interest to the
room, as does the pleasing mix of colors and textures.*

The antique blackamoor is a craft model, originally designed to gain accreditation for the èbénistes, a guild of furniture craftsmen in eighteenth-century France.

In France, a daybed is a perfect place to relax midday. This one is positioned so guests have a perfect view of the meandering creek at Charles's country cabin. Nicholas and Sadie love it for a little afternoon snooze.

An English Regency sterling tea tray rests on an elegant faux-bamboo lacquered stand. In front of the window is a Louis XVI marquetry table.

This sitting area is bathed in sunlight and features a French writing table flanked by a pair of Louis XV chairs and a small stool.

Symmetry is definitely at work in this sitting area. A zebra-skin rug anchors the space, featuring a large Empire table flanked by two period French chairs upholstered in a red toile.

The bar in this library was redesigned to look as antique as the French paneling that envelops the entire room. A pair of bookcases, fronted with old cabinet doors from France, frame the alcove. A carved panel, also found in France, hangs above the bar. (Previously published in Renovation Style magazine.)

Floral touches in the sunroom lead the viewer's eye to the gardens beyond. Almost everything in the room reflects nature.

ABOVE

This seating arrangement adjacent to the kitchen revolves around the lime-stone fireplace. With its twin sofas, comfortable chaise and large leather chair, the hostess can prepare food and still enjoy the company of guests. (Previously published in Renovation Style *magazine.)*

FAR LEFT

Decorated with an ornate majolica lamp and a patterned shade, and trimmed with fluted pleats, an old iron garden table becomes an important piece in the sunroom. A majolica plate continues the theme. (Previously published in Renovation Style *magazine.)*

This breakfast sitting area adjacent to the kitchen was originally the home's dining room. The cedar beams and moldings were added during a renovation. (Previously published in Renovation Style *magazine.)*

In France, the designer and his clients purchased an entire room of antique wood paneling ~ boiseries ~ shipped it home and put it back together like a jigsaw puzzle. It gives the room an authentic library appearance. (Previously published in Renovation Style magazine.)

LEFT

A painting by Pablo Picasso titled Tete d'Homme au Nez Vert *adds to the ambiance of this library without dominating the room. Beautiful fabrics chosen for their texture and color are enhanced by an exquisite antique Oriental rug.*

ABOVE

In the library of this California residence, the glass-and-iron table adds weight to the collection of antique furnishings.

The granite countertops in this home are accented by a hammered-copper sink, located under the kitchen window with cabinets on either side that house the microwave and built-in cappuccino machine.

A successful kitchen is one where host and guests feel perfectly coddled and comfortable. It is a space that functions both as a working kitchen and an informal living area ~ perfect for the kind of comfortable and casual entertaining people enjoy today.

Early on, I discovered the joy of visiting with my guests while meals were being prepared. I had built only one other kitchen and it featured a sitting area with two wing-back chairs. That meant that I usually had to stand at the stove to visit with my guests. When I moved to a historic saltbox-style home in 1987 and added a new kitchen, I knew I needed a comfortable seating area that accommodated six or eight people, which would allow me to enjoy my guests even more.

A kitchen is all about ease of cooking and entertaining. A neutral color scheme works well in many kitchens. Open shelving also offers the opportunity to display collections. My own home includes collections of blue-and-white porcelain, bovine portraits and Staffordshire cows and chickens.

In the mien of a French farmhouse, ceilings are often a focal point, as in one house where the ceiling was composed of beams with grape-stake fencing between them ~ salvaged fencing that was hosed down at high pressure, white-washed, then cut to fit the beams.

Another kitchen detail featured faux-stone wallpaper, complete with a chiseled-looking keystone of the date I moved into the home. In another home, an oak leaf-and-acorn-patterned wallpaper coordinated well with a bronze chandelier. In my weekend cabin, wallpaper that resembled barn siding was a rustic backdrop for framed tiles and pewter pieces. In one kitchen, old French exterior doors concealed kitchen necessities.

In a real French kitchen, there are no upper cabinets. I followed that design theme in building my French château-style home. China and silver were stored on shelves hidden behind two exterior doors, their glazed panes replaced by squares of an old mirror. To complete the non-kitchen look, the room was lighted with a pair of table lamps by the sink, illuminating a bronze and crystal chandelier.

A small kitchen in this California home became the breakfast room and an entire new kitchen was added. The cabinets, constructed of reclaimed wood that has been distressed, were custom made by Masters Fine Woodworks in Tulsa.

Simply Entertaining

My friends seem to savor the simple and easy way I entertain. I love to entertain simply and I have a fairly standard menu that includes tenderloin, brisket or chicken, Caesar salad, rice pilaf, French bread and wine. That menu allows me to fix things ahead so I can truly enjoy visiting with my guests. When it comes to desserts, there are no poached pears or peach tarts. I have one rule about the desserts served at a dinner party: They have to be chocolate or lemon, very fattening, and always extremely rich and heavy.

While the food that emanates from any kitchen is important, the ambience, the conversation, the comfort ~ and always the decor ~ are what entice guests to return again and again.

In the bovine-inspired kitchen, a center island with a handsome granite countertop incorporates a warming oven and storage cupboards. Charles used old French exterior doors to conceal ordinary kitchen necessities. (Previously published in Traditional Home *magazine.)*

A B O V E

An old butcher's shop sign hangs above the range hood in this kitchen, setting a bovine theme. The kitchen features a collection of pottery, Black Forest iron and terra-cotta cows. The wallpaper is "Acorns" by Greeff. (Previously published in Traditional Home *magazine.)*

R I G H T

Architectural salvage from France contributed greatly to the new look of this remodeled kitchen. An antique green door with fancy grillwork leads to the garage. Especially intriguing is the antique French armoire bonnet that covers the range hood. (Previously published in Renovation Style *magazine.)*

An eighteenth-century French Country, drop-leaf fruitwood table complements a nineteenth-century French corner banquette, a radassière in French, to create a perfect place to dine in the small breakfast nook of this kitchen. The red tole chandelier moves to a new house every time Charles does. In true French Country fashion, the open upper cabinets place collections in plain view.

Step into this comfortable open kitchen and you are instantly transported to Provence in France. Aged grape-stake fencing on the ceiling is outlined with reclaimed wood beams. The countertops are concrete. The center island is pear wood and was a period Louis Phillipe, nineteenth-century cashier stand.

ABOVE

Resembling a French country kitchen, the open shelves allow easy access to serving china and also provide a setting for collections of Staffordshire chickens and blue-and-white porcelain with origins in China, England and Spain.

FAR LEFT

An antique crystal apothecary jar becomes a showcase for a variety of wine corks.

The dining area in this contemporary kitchen includes comfortable seating. The fabric is a cheerful fruit and flower cotton print, "Bartlett," by Brunschwig & Fils. It is a bright, open space that reveals how French antiques, American crafts and sleek European-style cabinets can create a beautiful, flawless mix.

Although new, this home is true to its French Country origins. An antique butcher's sign hangs over the range hood. Early French chairs surround the old farm table. Reproduction floor-to-ceiling cabinets store dishes.

5

DINING ROOMS

A dining room is more than a setting for bountiful dining and lively conversation. It is as much a room to display collections as it is a place for elegant and gracious dining.

The same design principles that are used in other rooms come into play in a dining room. Fabrics for walls, draperies and upholstery are coordinated. Welsh dressers, commodes, matching buffets and English breakfronts are perfect stages to display collections ranging from Imari plates or blue-and-white porcelain to Staffordshire figures and antique tureens.

Like furnishings in other rooms of the house, dining room tables, chairs and accessories must be antique, or have the look of an heirloom, again preferably French, English or Provençal-style reproductions. Chandeliers are carefully chosen to highlight the rest of the room's furnishings, and fresh fruits and flowers are design staples.

In one home, the former library became the dining room, with a door removed and walled up to allow for better furniture arrangement. A chair rail, crown molding and an eighteenth-century wood mantel gave the room more definition and a comfortable French Country mood. A reproduction table was accented with two matching wing-back chairs, upholstered to match the padded fabric walls. Two French chairs with no sidearms were covered in antique leather, their backs dressed in checked silk. Nailhead trims accented all four chairs. A frequent element in my designs is the balanced mixture of two styles of chairs around a dining table, each featuring contrasting but color-coordinated fabrics to complement the room.

Another home, a small house in Tulsa, was transformed into a charming French Country cottage where the living and dining room share equal space. Fireplaces at each end of this main room establish the character of the space, with seating at one end and dining at the other. What makes this space so

LEFT

An antique French tapestry dominates the dining room in Charles's country cabin. An old farmhouse table is accented by Chippendale chairs, upholstered in "Senanque" by Pierre Frey, with a bench for additional seating. A companion view on page 5 shows the cabin dining area from the perspective of a second-story loft.

appealing are the furnishings and architectural pieces salvaged on a treasure hunt in flea markets and antique shops throughout France. One of the finds was an 1860s French side table with cabriole legs, which now serves as a coffee table. A wine and cheese table, flanked by matching upholstered chairs and set in a window alcove, adds another place for dining and conversation in this cozy cottage.

Auctions and trips to France furnished one client's dining room in a charming mix of French and Italian furnishings. An antique fruitwood dining room table anchors the room and graces a nineteenth-century Heriz rug. A set of eight Italian neoclassical, painted and parcel-gilt, eighteenth-century side chairs surround the gleaming table. The chandelier casts a soft glow on the paintings by Maximilien Luce and Camille Pissarro and a nineteenth-century painting of dogs.

FACING

A fruitwood dining table is the centerpiece of this room, complemented by an eighteenth-century French sideboard found in Bordeux. An auction yielded the eight Italian neoclassical, eighteenth-century side chairs as well as the nineteenth-century English paintings.

RIGHT

The backs of the dining chairs are painted with beautiful detail and are accented with gilt details.

*In this home, the dining area is at the opposite end of the living
room. The dining table is an antique French farm table with drop-
end leaves. The host chair is a nineteenth-century antique French
fauteuil covered in Brunschwig & Fils's "Ma Cabine au Canada,"
with a Brunschwig & Fils check on the back. The curtains are vin-
tage-style ticking in a sagebrush color named "Parasol" by Fabricut.
The double skirt fringe is by Tuscany Trimmings.*

BELOW

*Sometimes, a breakfast area can become a perfect place to read, especially if you
enjoy the morning newspaper. The bay window was custom built and showcases
an early porcelain stove. Although it was purchased in the French countryside,
the stove could be of Swedish lineage.*

BELOW

*An antique baker's rack is converted to a bar. Its location in the dining room
provides easy access for entertaining.*

*Although the dining table and chairs have been
featured in several of Charles's homes, the architecture and varied accessories in this one set an
altogether different mood. The painted-wood
candle chandelier adds a slightly rustic touch.*

ABOVE AND FACING

A nineteenth-century Swedish pine table is surrounded by nineteenth-century Directoire-style painted fruitwood chairs upholstered in "Menebres" by Pierre Frey. Blue-and-white Chinese-export porcelain and transferware plates are displayed on the walls around the room. The centerpiece on the table is a German Metlock tureen, one of Charles's most prized possessions. The curtains are a Chinese-style toile in blue and red.

You might call this "bay area" dining. It is a five-foot-deep bay in a hallway that runs across the back of Charles's former home. An antique bench is placed against the windows while eighteenth-century French Country chairs face a lovely view outside. The chairs are upholstered in "Carre Royal Rosso" by Clarence House and "Fountain Bleau" by Nancy Corzine. (Previously published in Traditional Home *magazine.)*

Nicholas and Charles relax in this small breakfast area of his Tulsa home. Antique chairs feature graceful carving on the back. They are upholstered in red-and-white toile. The settee cushions are "Eton Check" by Colfax & Fowler. The wallpaper is "Acorn" by Greeff and the curtains are "Scenes Champtres" by Pierre Frey.

A tole chandelier casts a glow over this special room, which has padded fabric walls and matching draperies in "Pasada" fabric by Pepe Penalver. The owners' collection of Imari is beautifully displayed in the Welsh dresser and on the walls. (Previously published in Renovation Style *magazine*.)

All of the furniture in this dining room is authentic French period. Antique candelabras and an epergne accent the table. The chairs are upholstered in "Chinoise" by Scalamandre. The French buffet des corps *features an eighteenth-century pewter collection.*

FACING

The wallpaper in the breakfast room of Charles's weekend retreat mimics rustic barn siding and creates a perfect backdrop for pewter pieces and framed tiles. Staffordshire chicken lamps rest on a nineteenth-century pine buffet, accenting a still life from the 1800s. Louis XVI chairs are covered in a small print, "Nimoise," by Travers. The wallpaper is by Scalamandre.

BELOW

Furnishings in this dining room are combined for their shape, color and texture. A contemporary glass and acrylic table with Italian-style chairs upholstered in cut velvet rests on an antique Persian rug. The painting is by American artist Gene Bavinger, circa 1990. Symmetry is maintained by the pair of painted Portugese wooden plant stands displaying antique bronze bouquets.

BELOW

The reproduction cast-stone fireplace is a twin to one on the opposite wall. Matching antique trumeau mirrors hang above. The Louis XV dining chairs were found on a shopping trip to France.

LEFT

A Louis XV dining table and chairs adorn this room, which features the sparkle of a bronze and crystal Baccarat chandelier. The walls and chairs are covered in a floral linen, "Musetta," by Decorator's Walk.

ABOVE

A nineteenth-century French butcher's table in wrought and cast iron with a marble top is a handsome piece in this eating area. The marble top tablescape includes pieces from the owners' vast collection of pink-and-white English ironstone.

BEDROOMS

6

A master bedroom suite is often dressed with rich textures and patterns, neutral tones, room-darkening draperies and touches of gold. The setting is always restful and soothing, providing an oasis at the end of a hectic day. Enveloping yourself in warm, inviting comfort is essential in the design of a bedroom.

As with the entryway and the living and dining room, I begin the design process with an important piece. For a bedroom it is usually fabric ~ often toile, which was Marie Antoinette's favorite print. And when you use toile, the more the better. I gravitate toward red-and-white patterns, usually with a cow or a herd of bovines in the pattern. Every room should have a touch of red, like a surprise. And every house should have a red room.

I seldom play favorites when it comes to rooms. I live all over a house. But I am unequivocal about color. Red is my favorite. Design 101 suggests you should never have a red bedroom because red is not considered a restful color. But I have never designed by rigid rules. I painted one of my bedrooms a rich red that was quite soothing.

Relaxing comfort is always at the heart of a bedroom design. But comfort took on a new meaning when I decided to spend a night in the guest room of my Dutch Colonial home. The room was a second-floor bed-and-bath suite, a tucked-away retreat dressed in elegant antique floral linens. The room was much warmer and so much cozier than my Empire-style master suite downstairs. It was the fabric that made all the difference. I began a revolution to ban the heavy velvet draperies, the leopard-print rug and a host of military collectibles that had been a mainstay of many of my personal bedroom designs.

That one-night change of scenery altered my perspective on the meaning of pure comfort in the bedroom.

I went totally toile. But instead of red-and-white, a restful brown-and-white pattern was used from floor to ceiling, including a window swag. Then

The guest bedroom in this home mixes plaids, checks and toiles to offer a warm, inviting atelier. The Provençal, carved antique headboard is upholstered in a red-and-green toile. A nineteenth-century two-drawer commode is next to the bed; on the opposite side is an early pine wine-tasting table. On the left wall, framed botanicals bring a touch of nature indoors.

painting the ceiling beams, crown molding, new library shelving, and window trim in a soft, creamy white enhanced the room's architectural allure.

Bookcases add warmth in any room. They also provide more space to display an abundant cache of reading material and treasured collections as well.

Existing seating was reupholstered and a new bedcover was designed in the matching toile linen. The print was a perfect backdrop for a mixture of French and English antiques featured in the room. A plaid comforter ~ a lucky estate-sale find ~ added contrast to the bed linens. A simple checked fabric was used to reupholster an antique wing chair, providing a restful counterpoint to the abundance of toile. Covering the walls and ceiling gave the effect of a canopy bed, a feeling of intimacy without the feeling of being closed in.

Most of the time, for my clients, I will follow the color scheme, architectural theme and prints and patterns used throughout the house. But my country cabin was a departure from that design principle. My bedroom in that home completely contradicted what I usually espouse for clients ~ that you should have continuity from one room to the next. Instead, I went from a light-filled Swedish house to a dark little log cabin for the bedroom.

The original plan was to whitewash the logs. But after living in the space during the winter while I was redecorating, it seemed quite cozy and I thought it might be "sacrilege" to paint the logs. In that same bedroom, there was another challenge to solve. The cabin's original front door was in the bedroom. To hide the door without going to the expense of removing it, an iron tester was added to the circa-1800 Edwardian bed so the headboard and fabric panels of blue-and-white check would conceal the door.

A favorite bedroom for me and for my dogs was in the Dutch Colonial home. The reason? The bedroom had a secret staircase to the kitchen ~ just perfect for my late-night snacks and the dogs' canine treats. I gave the dogs another special treat while designing the master suite for the French-style château. A secret door in the suite's closet allowed the dogs access to a fenced run outside. After all, dogs should be as pampered as clients.

LEFT AND RIGHT

In Charles's current bedroom, a painted eighteenth-century Italian commode is crowned by an antique Scottish portrait of a young man. Alongside is an early painted French case clock and a pair of English Adam-style elbow chairs upholstered in a Chinese-style toile. Charles used various paisley patterns at the window and on the bed.

Reproduction French bedside tables feature custom-made lamps topped with silk shades, illuminating the antique Staffordshire figures. An early portrait of a young French girl with her dog hangs above Nicholas, who naps everywhere.

The tester bed, fabricated by Charles's brother-in-law, Dale Gillman, is the showpiece of Charles's guest bedroom. It features beautiful iron scroll-work. Rather than use the traditional heavily draped panels and canopy, Charles left the frame unembellished to give the room a more open feeling. The azure color scheme is calming.

Pattern and texture abound with a mix of florals, stripes and checks. A small antique French chair and a needlepoint rug complete the room. The wallpaper is "Trianon" by Zoffany.

A fruitwood Louis XVI chaise longue *is a feature in this master suite. The cupboard was painted during the reign of Napoleon III and is accented with a pair of eighteenth-century Italian altar urns that have been transformed into custom lamps.*

Intricate carving graces the two doors of a fruitwood Louis XVI cupboard.

In the master bedroom, plum, aubergine and old gold provide a unique twist to the traditional toile. The French quilt is a purple floral with a reverse pattern. The wallpaper and matching draperies are "Après Midi" by Lee Jofa. The European quilted shams are "L'Oiseleur" pattern by Pierre Frey.

LEFT

A handsome four-poster bed by Patina, sans the traditional canopy, makes a striking statement in this Tuscan-style farmhouse. The vaulted ceiling creates architectural interest. The striped wallpaper is the perfect foil for the floral fabric used to upholster the chairs, "Roseville," by Bennison. Symmetry reigns above the bed with an artful placement of framed watercolors by Jim Steinmeyer.

ABOVE

This charming French-style bed is called a lit d'alcove, *or a bed in an enclosure of panels. Bookshelves and a small window add interest to this little girl's cozy sleeping area. An antique desk, small French chairs and a comfortable chair and ottoman would easily delight a young girl.*

ABOVE

A red-and-white color scheme, anchored by touches of black, is prominent in this bedroom. Tuffy enjoys a nap on the Empire-style bed, adorned with black-and-white pillows trimmed in red. A needlepoint pillow accents the bedside chair and a luxurious tassel hangs from the drawer knob of the antique bedside table, which features Charles's lucky santo. *(Previously published in* Traditional Home *magazine.)*

RIGHT

The carved-wood valances over the French doors began life as sideboards on an antique bed. The Federal-style bull's-eye mirror now hangs above the mantel in Charles's current living room. The curtain fabric is "L'Oiseleur" by Pierre Frey. *(Previously published in* Traditional Home *magazine.)*

FACING

The rustic stone fireplace and overstuffed chair from Charles's custom furniture line act as a magnet on weekends. It is his favorite place to curl up and read. The antique portrait of a British soldier over the mantel is one of his "instant ancestors."

ABOVE

Nicholas enjoys his perch on the 1800s Edwardian bed in Charles's weekend retreat. The bed curtains were added to help camouflage the cabin's original front door. The blue-and-white color scheme here is a darker shade than the paler blues used throughout the rest of the cabin. An antique Oriental carpet anchors the room.

Salles de Bains

BATHROOMS

7

OVERLEAF

An old metal washstand became the lavatory in this guest bathroom, featuring a Beaumanier limestone top and a hammered metal sink. The Irish mirror is gilt and ebony. The owners' collection of vintage European linens is reflected in the mirror.

A bathroom is one of the most fundamental and functional rooms in any home. But it should be designed with elegance and lavished with as much style as the major living areas. Colors should be rich and warm ~ always as comforting as a heated bath. And why not? We often start and end our day in these spaces of intimate refuge, so these rooms should be soothing to our soul.

The all-important vanity is the pivotal piece in bathroom design. Like major pieces in other rooms, it will usually be an antique ~ a marble-topped buffet, an antique campaign chest, a period room stove, even a radiator ~ all transformed into beautiful and workable vanities.

One nineteenth-century room stove that became a vanity and lavatory was covered with a Beaumanier limestone top and housed a hammered metal sink. Toilets are sometimes concealed in true French fashion with a closed stool ~ a French latrine with a hinged cane seat.

In one bathroom where space was at a premium, a vanity that had the look of an antique console was fashioned from a vintage iron radiator. Topped with easy-care marble, the piece was complete with its former cover serving as a decorative backsplash. The shower was hidden behind paneled doors to keep it from intruding on the furnished look of the bath. The tiny room now radiates a large welcome.

While unique vanities are frequently the showpieces in bathroom design, I used an eighteenth-century French zinc tub as the centerpiece in

LEFT

This half-moon lavatory features a marble top and a hand-painted sink. The wallpaper, "Tenture Flottante" by Brunschwig & Fils, is a rendition of classical drapery in the style of the Second Empire.

my weekend retreat. A nineteenth-century bamboo bookcase found a home in the same bathroom. It is one of the first antiques I ever bought and it is dear to me. The vanity in this bath was an antique chest, painted in the Swedish style by Tulsa artist Janet Davie to match the other Swedish furnishings and accessories I chose to dress the cabin. She also painted the decoration on the front of the tub. Walls were papered in a blue-and-white squirrel pattern, accented with eighteenth-century hand-colored prints and framed English botanicals.

Fixtures and accessories are often antiques, quite frequently the result of salvaging or recycling so a bathroom can be adorned with furnishings from the past. One bathroom featured an architectural window and a vintage bathtub, both found at the Paris Flea Market.

Towel storage also takes its creative cue from historical pieces. In one bathroom, a *bonnetière,* circa 1860, was used to store towels, soaps and lotions. In another, linen towels were hung from an antique wooden ladder. A Victorian English bamboo stand, circa 1860, became another fanciful display for bathroom linens.

Even the smallest bath can be accessorized with luxurious and exquisite fabrics, especially if the walls are being padded. I like to use curtains whenever possible in the bathroom, even if they adorn a shower rather than a window. A good design trick for keeping curtains inexpensive is to use modest fabrics, then trim with lush fringes and other unusual decorative accents.

Mirrors are usually ornate antique finds, accented with all kinds of sconces for illumination. Chandeliers and silk-shaded lamps cast their own special glow. Accessories may include fine porcelain plates or figures, vintage silver or crystal.

Whenever possible, I will include a final finishing touch ~ a chair that will have a place of honor in the bathroom. Of course, it must be of antique heritage, upholstered in fabric complementary to the walls and window treatments, sharing space with a needlepoint pillow or two.

For me, relaxing in the bathroom, savoring a space to unwind, is as important as anywhere else in the house.

A buffet was converted to a vanity in Charles's Tulsa bathroom. The room is accessorized with Napoleonic memorabilia, a **trumeau** *mirror, wall sconces and portraits.*

ABOVE

In the guest bathroom of his weekend retreat, an eighteenth-century zinc tub is a dramatic focal point. The blue squirrel-print wallpaper by Osborne & Little is a perfect backdrop for a portrait of ~ what else ~ a French chair.

RIGHT

At The Roost, gold embroidery gives a luxurious touch to bath towels housed in a bamboo chest. An ornate tassel adds a finishing touch.

FAR RIGHT

An old chest was used to create a new lavatory in Charles's weekend retreat. Toiletries take their place in a papier-mâché tray. Two antique apothecary jars add accents, as do linen hand towels.

ABOVE

A touch of humor is achieved in the guest
bathroom with a mirror framed in twigs
and a majolica figure sporting a bouquet
of daisies.

FACING

Located off a private courtyard, this bath is pure color and harmony. The toile,
"Gardenia" by Pierre Deux, is the perfect foil for the faux leopard rug and red leopard
velvet, "Zambezi Gros Point" by Brunschwig & Fils. The French bench in front of the dresser
lures the rag-doll cat, "Mr. Big," to bask in the sunlight. Framed botanicals hang above the
marble tub.

The Louis XV dressing table is a stage for the owner's collection of Staffordshire, fashion costume engravings, tole objects, and Victorian purses. Note the symmetrical arrangement of the sconces and framed pieces surrounding the mirror. The wallpaper is "Francesca" by Ralph Lauren.

FACING

In the man's bathroom, a masculine feeling is expressed with a marble-top Edwardian-style vanity with sterling accessories. The rich tones of the wood complement the wallpaper, "Monuments of France" by Stroheim and Romann.

Dressings

DRESSING ROOMS

8

OVERLEAF

This well-ordered shoe space reflects Charles's philosophy that there should be a place for everything in a dressing room. These shelves were arranged to match the different occasions where Charles might wear these shoes ~ from tomato soup–casual to black-tie.

D ressing well has always been important to me, and my dressing room reflects that interest in fashionable attire. But on the weekends at my cabin, while enjoying the restful, almost spiritual nature of the secluded setting, casual is my favorite way to dress. Through the years, I've come to realize the importance of a well-ordered dressing room for my clients and myself and the appropriateness of fashion in the scheme of one's personal, professional and leisure life.

While a dressing room is a very private atelier in most homes, this is never a room to scrimp on design. No room is ever too small or too private to have an abundance of style. Wallpapers can be lavish. Ceilings can have special beamed treatments. Carpets can coordinate beautifully with the furnishings. Shelvings accommodate not only fashion necessities in an extremely neat and tidy order, but also allow space for decorative displays.

If there is room, a center storage island can be an important feature in a dressing room, adorned with fashion accessories as well as favorite books, porcelain and silver-framed portraits of friends and family.

A dressing room should be as comfortable as the living room, sitting room or library, with antique bookcases, sofas and chairs making this a cozy, comfortable place to dress for the day or a special black-tie

LEFT

An antique towel bar holds this collection of ties for easy storage that is also functional. Humor is not forgotten, however. A Napoleonic hat is a bit of memorabilia that adds a touch of whimsy.

FACING

This dressing area in one of Charles's former homes not only reflects his penchant for neatness and organization, it intersperses his clothes with treasured memorabilia and books. The wallcovering by Stroheim & Romann features Italian words. (Previously published in Traditional Home magazine.)

occasion. In one dressing room, an antique cloverleaf footstool, covered in one of my favorite red paisley fabrics, was positioned next to the shoes in open cabinets and was accented with an antique tortoiseshell shoehorn for ease of dressing. For convenience, there was a table for a phone, a gleaming chandelier and antique hooks to showcase ties.

Two of my most exquisite dressing rooms were designed in a home for some long-standing friends and clients who had lived in a pure French home for twenty-three years and wanted a new home that was less formal, reflecting the French Country style they had come to love on trips to France. The stately, old two-story home they found in Tulsa seemed perfect for their changing lifestyle. But what it lacked was abundant closet space for the extensive professional and social wardrobe their lifestyle required. Building a new closet over the garage, and incorporating windows into the design solved the problem.

The new room never appeared as an add-on to those viewing the exterior of the home. The wife's dressing room was papered in red and white roses, a pattern called "Windsor Rose," and featured a series of two-tiered, open hanging shelves, a center storage island, a desk framed by a window and built-in armoires on either side.

Other amenities in this perfect dressing room include a built-in lavatory and a concealed ironing board. An antique secretary faces one wing of the closet, with a window that reveals a view of the pool and garden. Antique chairs, covered in fabrics to match the walls, front a table near a window overlooking the back lawn, offering a place for relaxation. The room's chandelier is an antique confection of metal roses, complementing the wallpaper and upholstery fabrics. The wife's dressing room features a place for everything, with everything in its place, probably the most wonderful, well-organized dressing room you will ever find ~ anywhere.

The husband's closet ~ the original small upstairs bathroom ~ is no less organized or decorated, from the Brunschwig & Fils red-and-white fabrics to the Empire furnishings and Napoleonic memorabilia on his dressing table.

The key to a dressing room that works for a particular lifestyle is culling, taking inventory of items left, breaking up the closet into manageable sections that fit specific and seasonal clothing groups. Creating two-tiered sections to double storage space, storing luggage in separate closet spaces, and storing out-of-season garments in cedar sections also make seasonal changeovers simple and easy.

LEFT & RIGHT

A granite-topped center island in this master closet features space for accessories and jewelry. Double bars in the clothing areas provide for a more efficient use of space and groups clothing in categories for easier dressing. The wallpaper and matching upholstery is the "Windsor Rose" pattern by Cowtan & Tout. The closet also houses a small lavatory and a dressing table with a built-in armoire on either side. (Previously published in Renovation Style magazine.)

Charles's current dressing room is Nicholas's favorite retreat. He sleeps there during the day when Charles is at work. The curtains are "Le Temps et L'amour" by Pierre Frey and complement the chairs, which are upholstered with "Les Vues De Paris" by Marvic. The carpet is by Stanton.

Antique crystal perfume bottles add a touch of elegance as they nest in a silver tray on an antique desk.

Détails

DETAILS

9

Nicholas, a King Charles spaniel, lives all over the house but actually prefers Charles's lap to other perches.

A large antique blackamoor stands next to a wine-and-cheese table with a m___ top. The blackamoor is a favorite among the designer's collections.

A great deal of the pleasure in decorating is found in the special details that comprise each room setting. While one unique piece can spark the creative design for a room, it is the finishing touches ~ those unusual details ~ that make a dramatic impact and create a lingering memory.

In my homes and those of my clients, it is a passion for collecting that allows me to add luxurious touches by using varied and extensive collections. Collections are created when you buy one thing you love, and then another and then you are addicted. By the third acquisition, you're off and running toward a collection. Then it becomes an all-consuming passion. Collections are vital to the final look of a room and they are essential to achieving the somewhat elusive, "lived in forever" look of French splendor and English comfort that defines the French Country theme.

Chairs were my first passion. I bought my first one when I was in college. Of course, it was French. And now, I can't stop collecting them. Each one is an individual. Perhaps I admire their self-centered qualities since only one person can sit in one chair at a time. That single French chair led to the purchase of a French bookcase. I paid it out. My father disapproved of that sort of thing, but I disobeyed him; my mother never told him. After that, I always had something in layaway. I remember saving lunch money while I was in college to pay out an armoire I adored.

My collections are both serious ~ blue-and-white Chinese export porcelain, English transfer pieces and treasured Napoleonic memorabilia ~ and whimsical. Numerous Staffordshire figures are a recurring detail through every home I have owned and many of those I have had the privilege to decorate for clients. There are also Staffordshire pieces that relate to farm animals ~ cows, chickens and especially dogs ~ expressed in large landscape paintings, stone

Brackets, whether of wood, stone or tole (tinplate) make great accent pieces in any room. In this entry, they create a stage for a pair of rare, antique, carved giltwood bouquets. But they can also easily display a family heirloom or a flea-market find too irresistible to leave behind.

OVERLEAF

A beautiful, eighteenth-century Italian chest with lyrical, curving lines is hand painted in a motif that matches the curves of the chest. It works well in any room and provides a distinctive feature in any setting.

pieces and needlepoint pillows, many of which I design and make myself. I love farm animals so much I think I'm really a farmer at heart.

Bird cages, blackamoors, antique French plates, allegorical tureens and Victorian Christmas ornaments all have been staples in my collecting repertoire. The source for many of these collections is the Paris Flea Market ~ or the Marché aux Puces, as the French say. I scour this inspiring setting for antique furnishings, unusual fabrics, accessories and architectural adornments that have a historical provenance or colorful lineage. I am particularly enchanted with the painted pine furniture often found there ~ pieces that have a slightly tired look but can be rejuvenated with fresh fabric combinations.

The rich detailing on this Empire chair is accented by a Bennison floral-patterned cushion.

holder, or a vase of tulips that mimic the flowers in a nearby painting.

Nestle fresh fruit in an Imari bowl on a dining room table adorned with fresh flowers. Let towels embroidered in gold script peek from an antique bathroom cupboard with wire mesh inserts. Candlesticks ~ always in pairs, like chairs ~ accompany fresh fruit and flowers. Put an orchid in a silver champagne cooler, with its reflection highlighted in a mirror. A mix of textures is also part of my affection for detail. This attention to point-counterpoint is seen in the choice of carpeting or antique rugs, the lush upholstery and drapery fabrics ~ con-

Many of my collections are mementoes of traveling. They are as important as the furnishings and accessories. It's exhilarating to showcase them in tablescapes on mantels, shelves, ledges, even the top of a baby grand piano. They are bountiful and engaging, and they bring wit and grace to a room's design.

Also essential is my love for the elegance of deep French and English carving, a detail that is often featured on a truly fine antique. I frequently use carved pieces, especially *panetières,* or French bread cabinets, as design accents. Many of these pieces express the beautiful craftsmanship of the seventeenth and eighteenth centuries when *èbénistes,* the skilled cabinetmakers near Paris, created exquisite pieces, often for royalty and wealthy clients.

The details can be as simple as crystal perfume bottles on a silver tray, antique linens crisply ironed and placed in a silver toast

trasting but complementary, the choice of elegant trims, fringes and tassels that grace everything from curtains and pillows to ottomans and lamps. Custom-made upholstered pieces are necessary in companionship with antiques because of their comfort level.

Pairing unusual fabrics with contrasting textures is also part of the French Country look and attention to detail. Use wool with silk, chenille with linen, damask with satin, and toile with heavy linen.

While the mix of periods and styles with contemporary architecture has long been a hallmark of my French Country signature, sometimes people have preconceived ideas about mixing contemporary architecture with traditional furnishings. But with fabric, texture, color, and the proper scale in furniture and accessories, along with the introduction of different centuries ~ antique and modern ~ traditional and contemporary can come together seamlessly in a pleasing union of periods and styles.

It's all in the mix ~ a mix that creates continental grandeur in every room design.

A pair of ormolu sconces frame the elegant **trumeau** mirror, which hangs over a beautiful French period commode. Fresh flowers are especially welcoming in an entry.

A period chest is ornate in itself, but accented by a richly carved, antique chair, candlesticks and fresh flowers in a pewter bowl, the vignette makes a rich design statement. "Mr. Big," however, is the real star.

Nicholas's friends Sister and Sadie take
an afternoon snooze on the porch
daybed at Charles's country cabin.

A canvas pillow, matching the hall wallcovering, accessorizes a daybed in this weekend retreat. It is upholstered in a stripe pattern, "Duncan Ticking" by Fabric Factory.

Needlepoint pillows are a great way to accessorize any setting. This one, featuring the image of a King Charles spaniel, covers a petite stool and has a place of honor next to a living room chair.

To embellish the guest bathroom in his country retreat, a Tulsa artisan turned a rather ordinary chest containing a lavatory into a conversation piece with her hand-painted designs.

A French chair with a cane seat and cushion in Pierre Frey fabric rests beside an antique French garden table with an iron base at Charles's country cabin. An iron urn filled with a stone bouquet accents the window, draped in another Pierre Frey fabric.

A favorite old iron candle-holder features a chicken as the centerpiece, complementing the Staffordshire lamp on a nineteenth-century pine buffet.

ABOVE

An eighteenth-century bureau cab-
inet displays a collection of blue-
and-white Chinese porcelain.
Filled with fresh roses, the vignette
has a festive air.

FACING

An antique daybed and nine-
teenth-century buffet des
corps give distinction to this
loggia and contrast beautifully
with the stone.

A collection of antique English and French stitcheries is arranged in a symmetrical fashion above an eighteenth-century chest adorned with matching lamps and small pots of miniature roses.

Elegant hand carving, reflecting themes from nature, featured many of the period French pieces that comprise part of the personality of French Country designs. The carvings easily become a focal point in any room.

In this client's living room, texture is created by layering fabrics, colors and patterns, and combining them with fringes and trims.

A trio of custom-made and elaborately fringed pillows finds a home on this sofa. Fringes and details are the frosting on the cake and a style signature of the designer.

BELOW

A beautiful pair of French bronze doré fire irons ~ a cat and a dog ~ sidle up to the bouquet of flowers on this coffee table.

Sunlight streams through French doors in this home, casting shadows on the antique painted French chair upholstered in "Crespières" by Pierre Frey.

This tablescape is quite international. It includes a Chinese porcelain vase, an antique Italian wood book stand with an early Italian oil portrait, a collection of English tortoiseshell, a Mexican santos and the footed part of a French ormolu cache pot.

*A bronze epergne doré
overflows with fresh flowers.*

*A collection of tortoiseshell
boxes creates an eye-catching
tablescape, with fresh roses
providing contrasting color
and texture.*

THE TEAM

CHARLES FAUDREE

INTERIOR DESIGNER

Celebrated for creating French-style interiors, Charles Faudree's work has been featured in leading shelter magazines, including *Traditional Home, Renovation Style, House Beautiful, Southern Accents* and *Veranda.* Seven homes designed by him, including his own, have been featured on the Home & Garden Television network. In 2002, he was chosen as one of the top 100 interior designers in America by *House Beautiful.* Charles Faudree Antiques and Interiors, established in 1980 in Tulsa, Oklahoma, is the base from which Charles travels worldwide to an international clientele.

JENIFER JORDAN

PHOTOGRAPHER

Texas-based Jenifer Jordan has been a renowned photographer for more than twenty years, specializing in interior/architectural photography. Her work has been included in *Better Homes and Gardens New Decorating Book, Second Home, Cottage Style, Real Life Decorating,* and *New Classic Style* among others. Her work also appears regularly in leading home shelter magazines including *Traditional Home* and *Renovation Style.*

NANCY E. INGRAM

PHOTO STYLIST/PRODUCER

Regional editor for Meredith Publishing since 1988, Nancy E. Ingram produces feature stories for all of Meredith's titles, including *Better Homes & Gardens, Traditional Home, Renovation Style, Country Home, Better Homes & Gardens Special Interest Publications* and *Better Homes & Gardens Books.* She resides in Tulsa, Oklahoma.

M. J. VAN DEVENTER
WRITER

M. J. Van Deventer is the author of *Western Design* and *Native American Style,* is a contributor to *The Encyclopedia of the American West, The Great Plains Encyclopedia,* and *Women of the Wild West,* and has had articles published in *Traditional Home, Renovation Style, Southwest Art, Cowboys & Indians, Cowboys and Country, True West,* and *American Cowboy.* She is director of publications for the National Cowboy and Western Heritage Museum, Oklahoma City, Oklahoma.

JIM STEINMEYER
INTERIOR RENDERER

Internationally known for his interior renderings, James Steinmeyer's work is featured in *Passion for Detail* with Charlotte Moss and *Russian Furniture: The Golden Age* with Antoine Cheneviere. He has had exhibitions in London at Colefax + Fowler, Paris at Emmanuel Moatti Gallery, Sydney at Martyn Cook Antiques, and the National Academy in New York. Born in Tulsa, Oklahoma, he now resides in New York City.

NICHOLAS
CHIEN

English-bred but French through and through, Nicholas, Charles's Cavalier King Charles Spaniel, has pawed himself to national recognition by twice appearing on the cover of *Traditional Home* and fifteen times within its pages. Nicholas has starred in two Home & Garden Television network presentations. He resides with his owner in Tulsa, Oklahoma.

Trade Secrets/Resources

California

Ann Dennis
2915 Red Hill Ave
Suite B106
Costa Mesa, CA 92626
714.708.2555
Country French Antiques and Reproductions

Melrose House
8454 Melrose Place
Los Angeles, CA 90069
323.651.2202

Jefferies Ltd.
852 Production Place
Newport Beach, CA 92663
949.642.4154

Stable of Antique Shops
Kathleen Stewart at Home
338 North LaBrea Ave
Los Angeles, CA 90036
323.931.6676

Lyman Drake Antiques
2901 S. Harbor Blvd
Santa Ana, CA 92704
714.979.2811
Warehouse of French Antique Furniture and Accessories

Terra Cotta
11922 San Vicente Blvd
Los Angeles, CA 90049
310.826.7878
Furniture Reproduction and Accessories

Tom Stansbury Antique
466 Old Newport Blvd
Newport Beach, CA 92663
949.642.1272

Uniquities
11740 San Vicente Blvd
Los Angeles, CA 90049
310.442.7655
Antique Furniture and Accessories on Consignment

New York

Elliot Galleries
155 East 79th St
New York, NY 10021
212.861.2222

George N. Antiques
67 East 11th St
New York, NY 10003
212.505.5599

Herbert De'Forge
1193 Lexington
New York, NY 10012
212.744.1858

John Rossellie
523 East 73rd St
New York, NY 10021
212.772.2137

King Antiques
57 East 11th St
New York, NY 10003
212.253.6000
212.674.2600

Royal Antiques
60 East 11th St
New York, NY 10003
212.533.6390

North Carolina

Ryan & Company
384 Hwy 107 S
Cashiers, NC 28717
828.743.3612

Oklahoma

Antique Warehouse
Dale Gilman
2406 E 12th St
Tulsa, OK 74104
918.592.2900
Antique Furniture, Lamps, and Light Fixtures

Cisar Holt
1609 E 15th St
Tulsa, OK 74120
918.582.3080
Lamps, Reproduction French and English Furniture

Royce Meyers Gallery
1706 S Boston
Tulsa, OK 74119
918.582.0288
Paintings and Prints

Sam Spacek
8212 E 41st St
Tulsa, OK 74145
918.627.3021
English and French Antiques

S.R. Hughes
1345 E 15th St
Tulsa, OK 74120
918.582.4999
*Contemporary, Asian & Classic Mix of Old
and New*

T.A. Lorton
1345 E 15th St
Tulsa, OK 74120
918.743.1600
Accessories, Lamps, and Fine Linens

Tennessee

A Little English
4554 Poplar Ave
Memphis, TN 38117
English Antique Furniture and Accessories

Catherine Harris
2115 Merchants Row
Germantown, TN 38138
French and English Antiques

Texas–Dallas

Country French Antiques
1428 Slocum St
Dallas, TX 75207
214.747.4700
Country French Furniture and Accessories

George Cameron Nash
150 Dallas Design Center
1025 N Stemmons Freeway
Dallas, TX 75207
214.744.1544
Fine Furniture and Antiques

Joseph Minton
1410 Slocum St
Dallas, TX 75207
214.744.3111
French Antique Furniture and Accessories

The Mews
1708 Market Center
Dallas, TX 75207
214.748.9070
Stable of Antique Shops

Pierre Deux
415 Decorative Center
Dallas, TX 75207
214.749.7775
French Country Furniture Reproductions

Uncommon Market
2701 Fairmont
Dallas, TX 75201
214.744.3111
English Antiques and Accessories

The Whimsey Shop
1444 Oak Lawn
Dallas, TX 75207
214.745.1800
French Antiques and Accessories

Donald Embree Antiques
1115 Slocum
Dallas, TX 75207
214.760.9141
French Antique Furniture and Accessories

Texas–Houston

Area
3200 Shepherd
Houston, TX 77098
713.528.0220

Brian Stinger
2031 West Alabama
Houston, TX 77098
713.526.7380
French Antiques and Accessories

Joyce Horn Antiques
1008 Wirt Rd
Houston, TX 77055
713.688.0507
French and English Antiques

Paris

Paris Flea Market
Marché aux Puces
Saint-Ouen Flea Market
Porte de Clignancourt